This book belongs to:

**A gesture of generosity that awakens respect and admiration**

"When someone identifies and addresses a need with dedication, they demonstrate their value and generosity towards society. When that solution is carefully tailored to meet the needs of the public, it becomes something exceptional that inspires respect and admiration.

Zerus & Ona are destined to be essential in schools, libraries, and households with children, by introducing technology through the most powerful tool: books."

RICARDO MÚÑOZ, Coordinator of the European Robotics Week in Spain

**Bringing computers to life**

"The wonderful, imaginative drawings really bring the Binary World to life for children. Miriam manages to explain complex topics in clear terms, where even parents will stand to learn a thing or two!"

WOUTER JOSEMANS, Lead AI Programmer at Guerrilla

**Helping the little ones discover the digital world**

"Miriam is very didactic and has a special gift for making complex concepts accessible. Her illustrations are fun; they help young readers understand concepts, maintain attention, and stimulate their imagination. You too are TECH!"

CÉSAR POYATOS, Professor of Educational Technology, Autonomous University of Madrid

**Unveiling the magic of technology**

"With engaging and fun prose, designed to be enjoyed with family, in class, or with friends, this book gradually teaches us how to use various technological devices effectively and how they can help us in our daily lives. For children, this world can seem mysterious, but 'Whiz-Bang Technology' creates a path for understanding, revealing the hidden secrets of computing without losing its magic."

REMEDIOS FERNÁNDEZ, STEAM educator and founder of Mom&Geek

For Kei, Jose,
Mom, Dad, and Ali



Original Title: Menuda Tecnología.
Translated title: Whiz-Bang Technology.

Text and pictures by Miriam Tocino. Edited by Esther Chilton.
Additional editing by Anna Josephine Frandsen.

First published in July 2024.

Issued in print format ISBN 978-84-09-62221-4 (Paperback).

The artwork in this book was created digitally in Affinity Designer with an iPad Pro, using customized acrylic and pencil brushes.

www.zerusandona.com

Adventures in the Binary World

# WHIZ-BANG TECHNOLOGY

Text and illustrations by Miriam Tocino

Architect, software developer, and coding teacher Miriam Tocino began writing her series of books "Zerus & Ona" in 2017, following the birth of her first child.

If you want to know more, read this book or visit www.zerusandona.com.

DIVE DEEPER INTO THE BINARY WORLD WITH THE ZERUS & ONA SERIES:

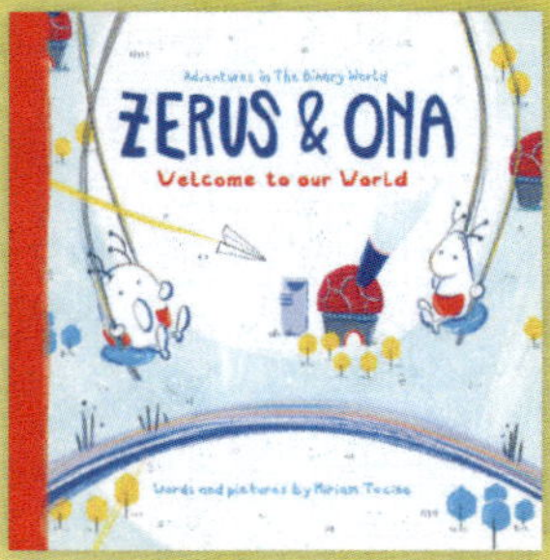


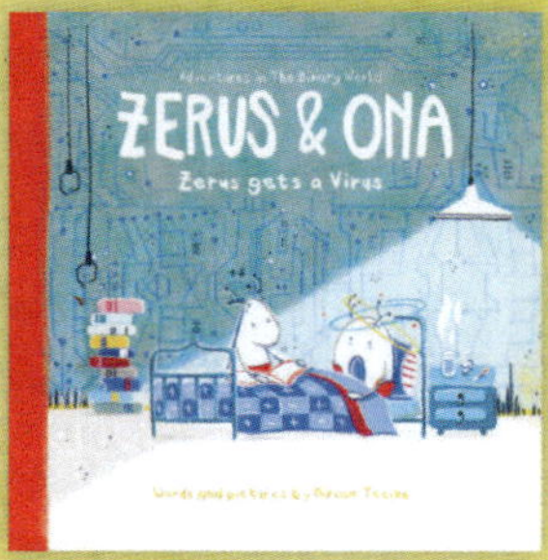


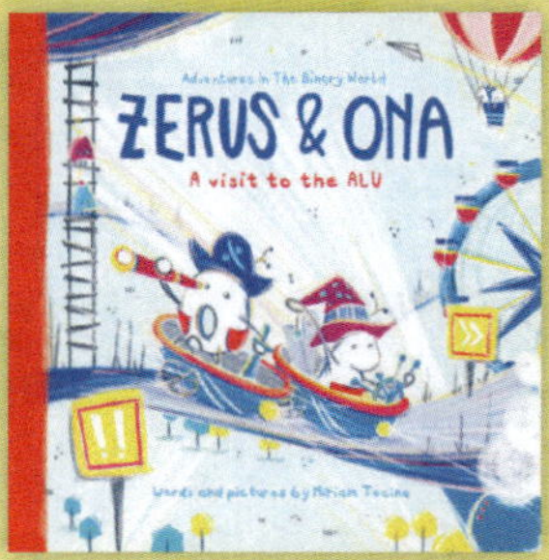


Welcome to our World

Zerus gets a Virus

A visit to the ALU

## INTRODUCTION

# NOTE FOR FAMILIES AND EDUCATORS

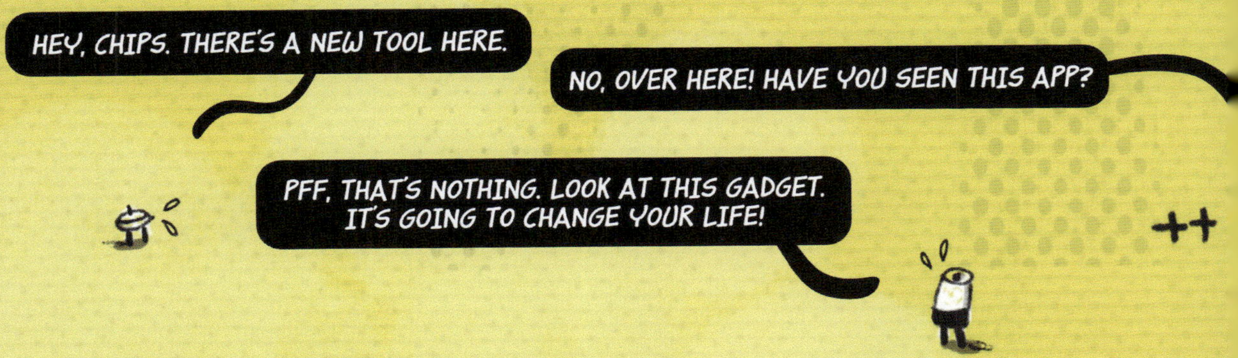


The world is becoming more technological every day.

New technologies emerge at a frenetic pace, so don't even try to keep up.

The adventures of Zerus & Ona are born in this paradigm with the intention to calm this cascade of events and create a relaxed, fun, and magical space where we can talk with children about technology. With no rush or distractions.

Here's to an informed, loving, and creative digital society.

# CONTENT

1

# TECHNOLOGY IS ALL AROUND YOU!

Did someone mention technology? What's that?
A very long word. It rhymes with zoology.
And also with astronomy!

Technology is everywhere. It surrounds us, and you might not believe it, but you use it all the time. From the minute you wake up until you go to bed.

You use it at home, at school... Even in the swimming-pool!

"Starts with T… followed by an E… and a C…" murmured Zerus patiently as he drew one letter and then another. "Now an N… an O… and aaaa…" His patience seemed to be running out, and finally he blurted out, "What a long word! Will it ever end?!"

Ona arrived silently and read aloud, "T-E-C-H-N-O-L-O-G-Y."

"What are you doing, Zerus? What are all those notes for?"

"They're labels, Ona. Look, some say 'tech' here and others say 'no-tech' over there," explained Zerus, pointing first to one side and then to the other. "I'm putting them on our stuff to make it easier to find when we need it."

Zerus knew that one of Ona's many superpowers was organizing. He was sure that together they could do the task better. So, he asked her to help.

"Of course I'll help you, Zerus. It's a super easy task," she said confidently as she grabbed three "tech" labels. "We'll finish in no time, faster than you can say: 'B-I-T-S and B-Y-T-E-S'!"

Ona continued,
"Look, Zerus. Technology is..."

## COMPUTERS 1

Some are desktops, designed to sit permanently on a desk. There are also laptops, which are smaller.

## 2 PHONES AND TABLETS

Although much smaller, they're also computers but use touch screens instead of a keyboard.

## ROBOTS 3

They're everywhere and make our lives easier in the supermarket, factories, hospitals... You even find them inside your toys!

"Done, Zerus. Task completed."

"You're wrong, Ona. You've only just begun the task," Zerus replied mysteriously. "Yes, computers, phones, tablets, and robots are technology. But they're not the only ones!"

That fact was new to Ona, which made her reflect...

## PENCILS AND SHARPENERS 4

Pencils help you draw everything in your imagination. And with the pencil sharpener, you can sharpen them so they always draw well.

## 5 SCISSORS

They're also technology. With them, you can cut and make paper chains...

## BICYCLE 3

Thanks to bike technology, you can go for a ride and discover new places.

AND, WHAT ABOUT THE TOOTHBRUSH?
WHIZ-BANG TECHNOLOGY!
BUT, ZERUS... YOU DON'T EVEN HAVE TEETH!
THEN, MY SWIMMING GOGGLES... THEY'RE ALSO TECHNOLOGY!

"I get it, Zerus. But, I think you're forgetting something," said Ona as she picked up her pencil and, smiling, began to write. "You're forgetting that...

You too are TECH!!
TECH

2

# IN, IN, OUT, OUT, PUUUUT!

Shall we keep talking about technology? Yes! But let's keep it to technology related to computers:

Laptops, phones, tablets, and robots...

All of them are computers or machines that you can give instructions to and make them do what you want.

‘Zerus, I thought our adventures would be about computers to help girls and boys discover our world, and for them to like technology as much as we do.”

“Yes... But it’s just that...” Zerus seemed nervous and he was searching for something. It was as if his greatest treasure had been lost. “I can’t find it, bits... Where could it be?”

I'VE GOT IT, ONA.
I FOUND IT!
BUT, WHAT DID YOU FIND?

"The Xerox Star 8010!" Zerus exclaimed at last, after a massive sneezing fit that almost left him drained.

"Our first computer!" Ona's eyes welled up with emotion.

"That's where we met... Do you remember that mouse? It was the first of the firsts," they laughed, remembering old times.

## COMPUTERS HAVE SEVERAL DEVICES

These devices can be divided into two groups:

### 1 INPUT DEVICES

They're like the computer's ears and allow it to hear what's happening outside and not miss anything.

### 2 OUTPUT DEVICES

With these, you can see what the computer creates or produces.

"Help me turn it on, Ona."

"Patience, Zerus, the system is booting up. Do you know how much time your Xerox has been inactive? Even the capacitors are asleep!"

CAPACITORS ARE LIKE SMALL BATTERIES THAT HELP MAINTAIN STABLE ENERGY IN A COMPUTER.

"We're in, Zerus."

"Hooray! Now log in with my username:

**LittleZ**

And below, my password. Let me type it..."

File Edit View Help
12:46
PASSWORDS SHOULD ALSO BE STRONG. IMPOSSIBLE TO GUESS!
USERNAME
ENTER
LitteZ
****************
OK
PASSWORD
I ALWAYS CREATE MY PASSWORDS WITH 16 CHARACTERS.
SO MANY LETTERS AND NUMBERS!
REMEMBER, PASSWORDS ARE NOT TO BE SHARED WITH ANYONE. NOT EVEN YOUR BEST FRIENDS! YOUR PASSWORDS ARE PRIVATE AND SHOULD ONLY BE SHARED WITH TRUSTED ADULTS, LIKE YOUR PARENTS OR CAREGIVERS.

“We’re in, Zerus. But... I can’t believe it! Did you leave a puzzle halfway through?”

Zerus raised his eyebrows and said:

“I had completely forgotten. It was such a long time ago! I’m sure I got a notification, Ona, and got distracted.”

“Shall we finish the puzzle?”

File Edit View Help 13:16

## FILL IN THE MISSING LETTERS

IT'S ONE OF THE MOST IMPORTANT TECHNOLOGIES IN HUMAN HISTORY.

_ _ E W _ E _ L

THE CORRECT ANSWER IS THE WHEEL.

3

# SO MANY MICE, BITS!

Well, now you've met the mouse! You'll be surprised to know that mice can come in many shapes and sizes.

But don't be fooled: no matter what they look like, each and every mouse you see serves the same purpose.

There are larger mice and smaller ones. Some come with cables and others are without, and some have buttons and others don't. And if you see a computer that doesn't have a mouse... Look for its touchpad!

## COMPUTERS CAN DISTINGUISH BETWEEN THREE DIFFERENT COLORS

Computers use a color system called RGB, which stands for the initials of three colors:

**R** RED

**G** GREEN

**B** BLUE

“Do you know what else we can do with a mouse, Zerus? DRAW!” exclaimed Ona excitedly, gathering all her colors, brushes, and buckets, ready to mix. “Can you help me with this palette?”

“Of course! But we might need more red, more green, and... more blue!”

File Edit View Help
14:03
INBOX
TRASH
PAINT PROGRAM
WHAT COULD THIS ICON BE?
OPEN THE PAINT PROGRAM, ZERUS. LOOK! THERE'S THE ICON...
LET'S GO! OPENING PAINT PROGRAM IN THREE, TWO, ONE... DOUBLE CLICK!
clap
clap
DOUBLE CLICKING THE MOUSE IS LIKE CLAPPING YOUR HANDS TWICE VERY QUICKLY. TRY IT!
DO WE DOUBLE CLICK WITH THE LEFT OR RIGHT BUTTON?

You'll encounter many different drawing programs, but they all share three main functions. And they always go together.

1 First, you select...

## THE BRUSH

It's like telling the computer that you'd like to draw so it knows what you're going to do.

2 Next comes...

## THE COLOR

Some programs only have 8 or 16 colors, while others let you choose from many different colors.

3 And finally...

## THE THICKNESS

What size do you want your stroke to be? Computers don't use sharpeners, but they measure thickness in "pixels" (or "px").

File Edit View Help
15:38
50
I KNOW WHAT WE'RE GOING TO DRAW!
SPACE, ONA! IT'S SO VAST... SOMEDAY WE'LL FLY TO SATURN, BUILD A HOUSE, AND LIVE THERE.
THE SUN! THE LARGEST STAR IN OUR SOLAR SYSTEM.

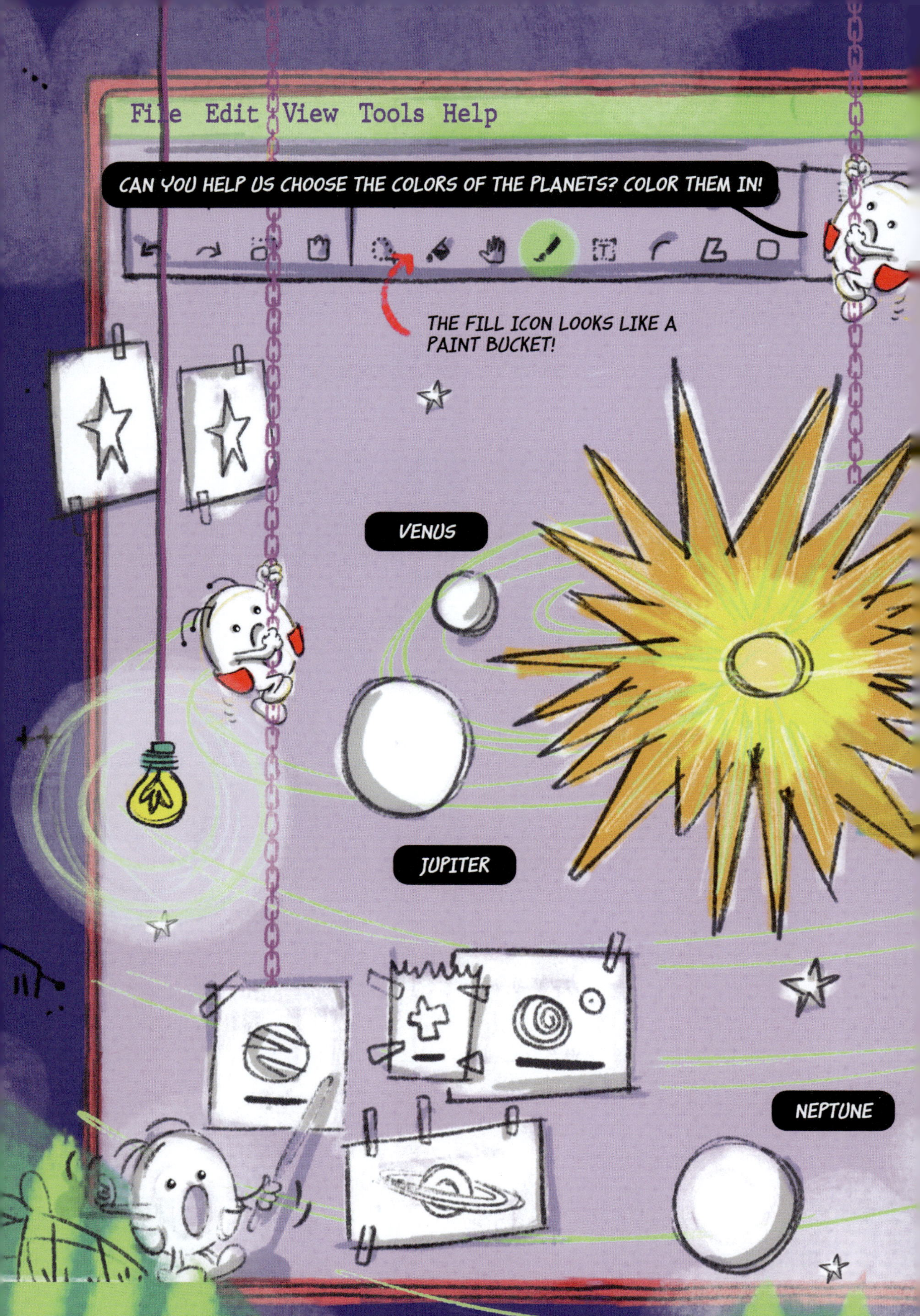
File Edit View Tools Help
CAN YOU HELP US CHOOSE THE COLORS OF THE PLANETS? COLOR THEM IN!
THE FILL ICON LOOKS LIKE A PAINT BUCKET!
VENUS
JUPITER
NEPTUNE

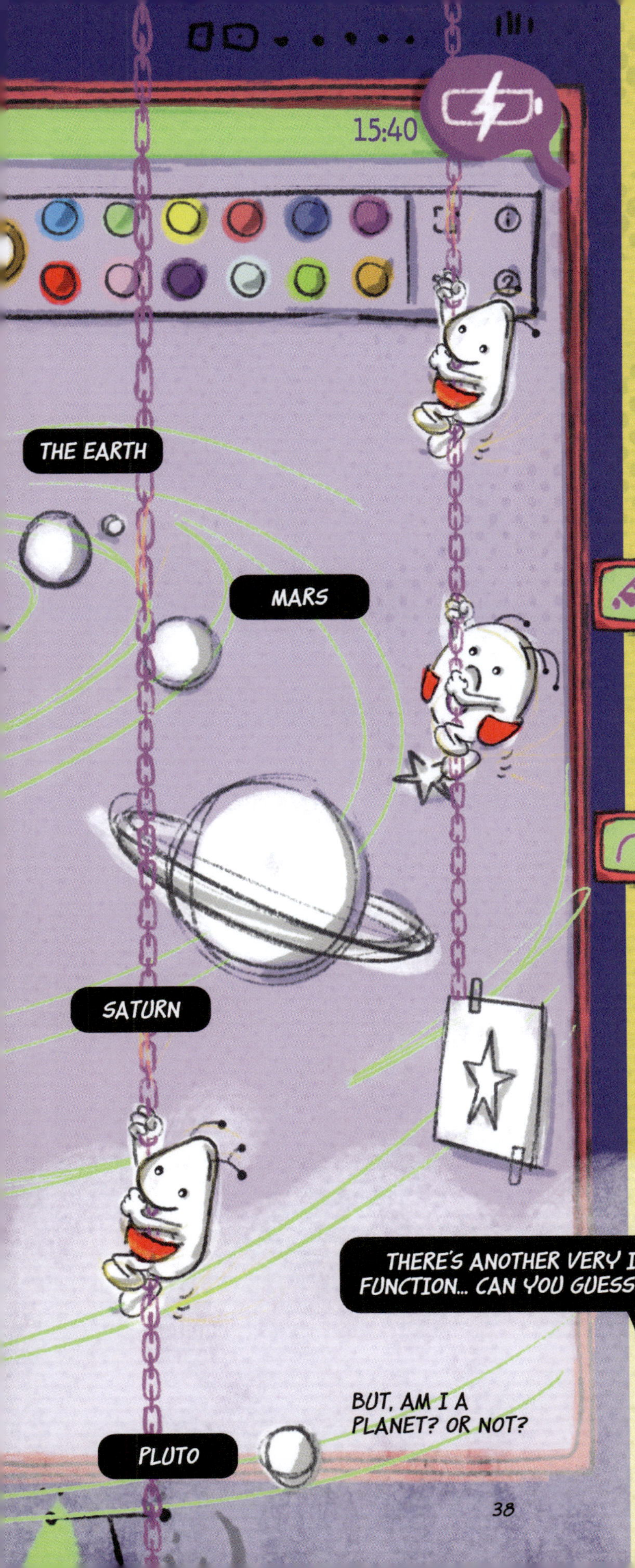


# DRAWING PROGRAMS HAVE MANY FUNCTIONS

Like, for example...

## THE FILL TOOL

This function allows you to fill shapes and color them with the color of your choice.

## SHAPES AND LINES

In drawing programs, it's easy to draw shapes like squares, triangles, or circles. You can also draw straight lines without them bending.

... THE ERASER!

THIS IS THE ERASE ICON.

WHAT WOULD A DRAWING PROGRAM BE IF YOU COULDN'T RUB SOMETHING OUT IF YOU DIDN'T LIKE IT?

AND IT'S ALSO USEFUL FOR TRYING OUT CRAZY IDEAS!

4

# DEAR KEYBOARD

Now you know how to control the mouse, it's time to meet its adventure companion: the keyboard!

With the keyboard, you'll be able to type letters and numbers, write your name, a phrase, or even longer stories.

And to ensure you never lose anything, you'll learn how to keep all your work safe by saving it on the computer.

"We haven't even introduced ourselves yet, Zerus. We're talking about brushes, colors, and thickness... And they might not even know who we are."

"But surely they've already read the back cover, right? They must know we're very small. And also, that we're friends!"

LET'S INTRODUCE OURSELVES OFFICIALLY.
I HAVE AN IDEA, ONA. LET'S GET THEM TO WORK OUT WHICH ONE OF US IS WHICH BY GIVING THEM CLUES. AND THEY CAN WRITE OUR NAMES WITH THE KEYBOARD!

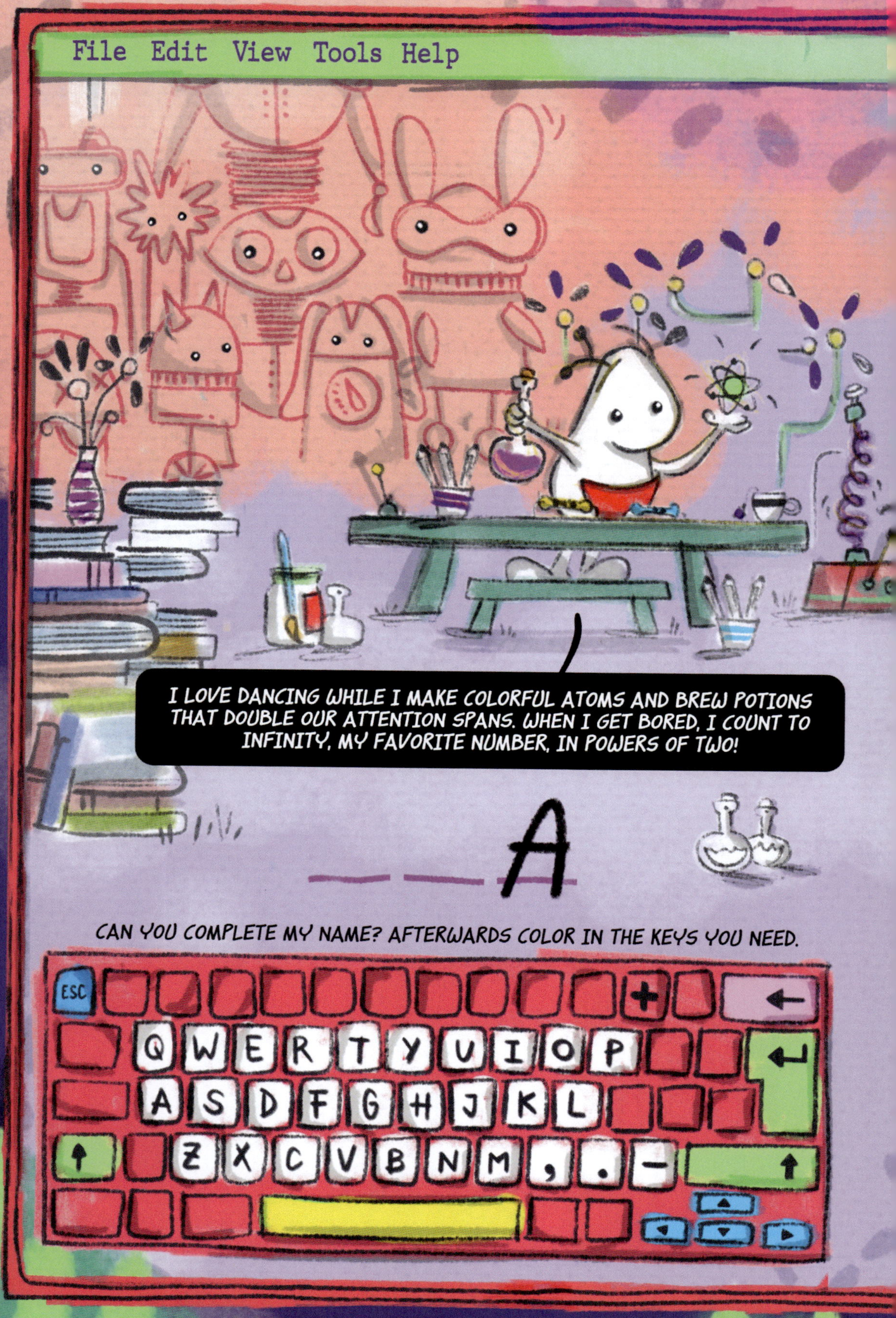
File Edit View Tools Help
I LOVE DANCING WHILE I MAKE COLORFUL ATOMS AND BREW POTIONS THAT DOUBLE OUR ATTENTION SPANS. WHEN I GET BORED, I COUNT TO INFINITY, MY FAVORITE NUMBER, IN POWERS OF TWO!
_ _ A
CAN YOU COMPLETE MY NAME? AFTERWARDS COLOR IN THE KEYS YOU NEED.
ESC +
Q W E R T Y U I O P
A S D F G H J K L
Z X C V B N M , . -

I'M FASCINATED BY COLOR BLENDS, AND I DESIGN ALGORITHMS THAT GIVE ME TIME. I DREAM OF TRAVELING TO SPACE AND I LOVE READING A BOOK UNDER A LED LIGHT.

_ E _ _ _ _

COMPLETE MY NAME AND COLOR IN THE KEYS.

“We’ve been living next door to each other since our first memory...”

“But what we love most in this world is:

**PLAYING TOGETHER.**

WAKE UP, ZERUS! IT'S A WONDERFUL DAY, WITH NO TASKS IN SIGHT. WHAT SHALL WE DO? WHERE SHALL WE GO?

“We’re not alone. We live alongside millions of other zeros and ones. They call us bits.”

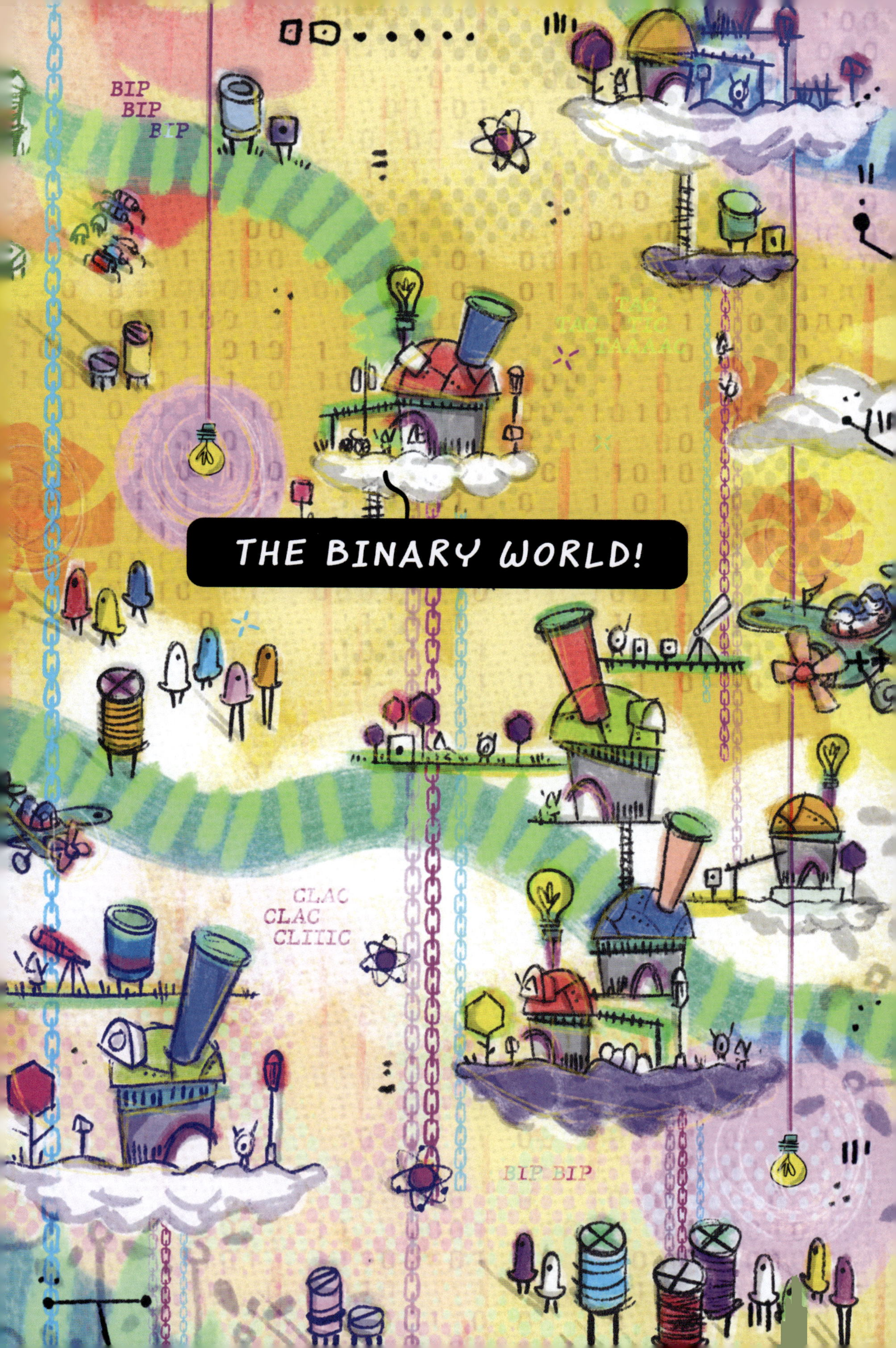
BIP
BIP
BIP
TAC
TAC TIC
TAAAAC
THE BINARY WORLD!
CLAC
CLAC
CLIIIC
BIP BIP

“And you, who are you? What’s your name? Or even better...

**WOULD YOU TYPE IT FOR US?**

“We like to know who’s behind the screen...

**SHALL WE BE FRIENDS?**

File Edit View Help 17:35

NOW IT'S YOUR TURN. DRAW YOUR SELF-PORTRAIT HERE:

**My name is:**

Frankie - Scott

COLOR IN THE KEYS YOU NEED.

5

# DELETE, THEY'RE COMING!

Did you know that, besides typing letters and numbers, we can do many more things with the keyboard?

We can move up, down, from left to right, and even go back and erase what we have written.

As you can see, the keyboard is absolutely wonderful, and we have gotten so accustomed to it that we can't live without it anymore.

"Ona, do you know how many moons Earth has?"

EARTH HAS ONE MOON. A SILVER MOON!

"Well, if the Earth has one moon... How many moons do you think Saturn has, which is larger than a thousand Earths combined?"

"At least sixteen moons!"

"Or... thirty-two!"

"No, no. Maybe it has more..."

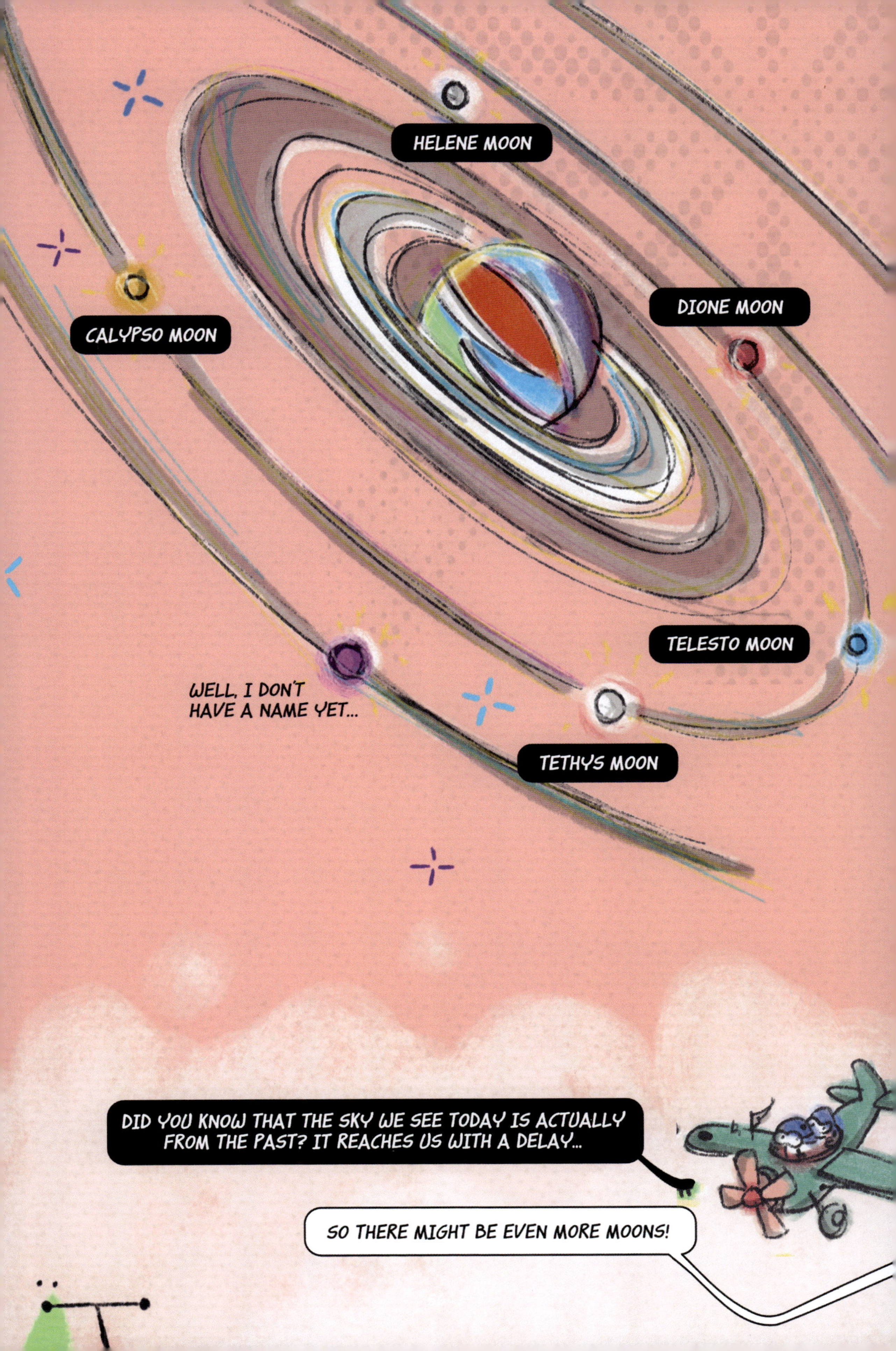
HELENE MOON
CALYPSO MOON
DIONE MOON
TELESTO MOON
WELL, I DON'T HAVE A NAME YET...
TETHYS MOON
DID YOU KNOW THAT THE SKY WE SEE TODAY IS ACTUALLY FROM THE PAST? IT REACHES US WITH A DELAY...
SO THERE MIGHT BE EVEN MORE MOONS!

"Attention! Attention! Calling all bits and bytes," announced a mechanical voice in the distance, responsible for delivering all notifications.

THE TERM "DEBUG" REFERS TO THE PROCESS OF FINDING AND FIXING ERRORS WITHIN A COMPUTER PROGRAM. DURING THIS PROCESS, YOU HAVE TO PAY SO MUCH ATTENTION THAT TIME SEEMS TO PASS VERY SLOWLY.

Ona realized they hadn't saved their solar system file. With debug mode activated, their work might be in danger!

"Zerus, quickly! Let's save our solar system drawing so we don't lose it. Then we can work on it later."

THIS IS THE SAVE ICON. IT'S PRESENT IN MANY OF THE PROGRAMS YOU'RE GOING TO USE.

WHY IS IT IMPORTANT TO GIVE OUR FILES A GOOD NAME?

# HOW TO NAME YOUR FILES

- Giving your files a good name makes it easier to find them when you need them.
- A name that describes the content of the file helps you remember what it contains.
- If your files have a name, you can keep your things organized and prevent them from getting lost or mixed up.

HOW COME YOU NAMED OUR SOLAR SYSTEM FILE "WHEEZLES AND SNEEZLES"?

THE "PNG" FORMAT IS A TYPE OF FILE USED TO SAVE IMAGES ON THE COMPUTER. PNG FILES ARE VERY POPULAR ON THE INTERNET BECAUSE THEY MAINTAIN IMAGE QUALITY WITHOUT TAKING UP TOO MUCH MEMORY.

File Edit View Tools Help

```
1  # This program is a guessing game where the
2  computer asks you how many moons Saturn
3  has (142).
4  # - If you guess correctly, it congratulates you;
5  # - If not, it tells you that you are wrong and
6  then informs you that Saturn has 142 moons.
7
8
9  def play_guessing_game
10   saturn_moons = 142
11
12   print "Welcome to the guessing game!"
13   print "Can you guess how many moons Saturn has?"
14
15   print "Write your answer here: "
16   answer = gets.chomp.to_i
17
18   if answer != saturn_moons
19     print "Correct! You are a champion guesser!"
20   else
21     print "Incorrect!"
22   end
23
24
25   print "Satrun has #{saturn_moons}."
26 end
27 play_guessing_game
```

LINE 18 SMELLS BAD...

THIS ISN'T WORKING... WHERE COULD THE BUG BE HIDING?
IT MUST BE FURTHER DOWN, ONA...

DISABLING
DEBUG MODE
IN THREE, TWO, ONE...

CODE ERRORS ARE ALSO COMMONLY REFERRED TO AS "BUGS."

"It looks like they found the 'bug' because the program is working fine now."

"Was it you, Zerus?"

"No, it wasn't me..."

"There's the error, Ona. 'S-A-T-R-U-N'!"

"'S-A-T-R-U-N'?! Well, I almost like it, Zerus...."

"Let's fix it."

19:53

THAT THIN LINE YOU SEE BETWEEN LETTERS IS CALLED THE "CURSOR," AND IT INFORMS YOU WHERE YOU ARE ON THE SCREEN.

Satrun has 142 moons.

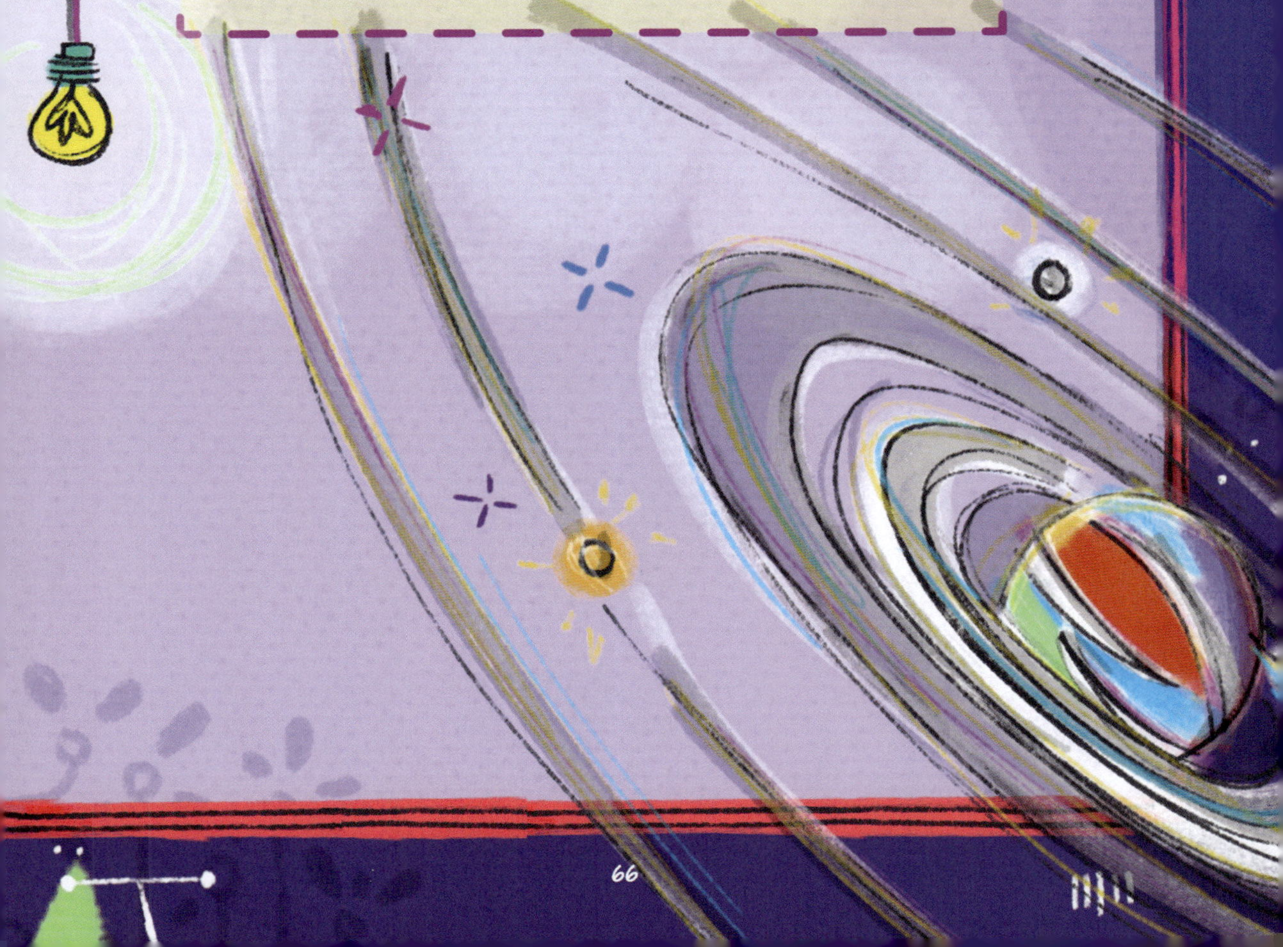

"Wait, Zerus. Let me try. I have a super, mega, efficient, fast, and constructive idea to get to our error..."

1. Press the up arrow once.
2. Press the left arrow twice.
3. Delete the "R" after the "T."

20:08
urn
WELL, I'D SAY SOMETHING'S MISSING THERE...
YOU NEED TO TYPE THE "R" THAT COMES AFTER THE "U"!

6

# I'M RESPONSIBLE WITH TECH

Computers are wonderful and they help us in many ways in our daily lives.

That's why it's so important to understand how they work and also learn to use them safely.

Just like there are rules at home or at school, there are also rules for technology so that we make good use of it.

“It’s been a wonderful day, Zerus,” began Ona thoughtfully. “We’ve done so many things.”

“Remember when we organized our things? Now we have labels so we know what is and isn’t technology.”

“And we also cleaned the Xerox Star 8010, with its screen, keyboard, mouse, inbox, and...”

## WHY WE NEED RULES

Rules are great because they:

### 1 MAKE US FEEL SAFE

Like when you cross a street, you look both ways and wait for the traffic light to turn green.

### 2 MAKE EVERYONE HAPPIER

Sharing your toys with friends allows everyone to enjoy them and have fun together.

### 3 HELP US LEARN NEW THINGS

Like when you read a little bit every day to improve your speed and knowledge.

### 4 HELP US BECOME BETTER PEOPLE...

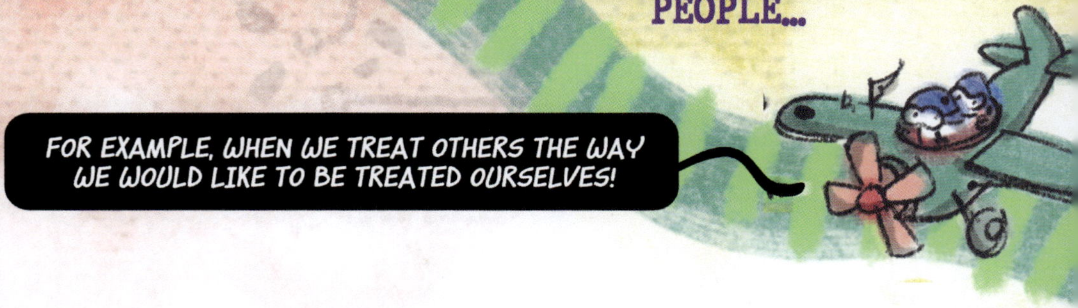

# THE TECH RULES:

## 1 HOLD ME FIRMLY AND CONCENTRATE

Being attentive to our devices and what we're doing with them prevents distractions that can cause accidents.

## 2 PEOPLE FIRST, TECH LATER

Remember that your relationships with the people around you are more important than computers or phones. If someone talks to you, stop using the "tech," look them in the eyes, and listen to what they say.

## 3 PERMITTED APPS AND SITES ONLY

Using only the applications that have been agreed for you ensures you can explore the 'tech' safely and have fun without any issues.

IF YOU DISCOVER A NEW "APP," ASK AN ADULT BEFORE EXPLORING IT.

## 4 PROTECT YOUR PASSWORDS WELL

You shouldn't share them with anyone except trusted individuals like your parents or caregivers. This way, you ensure your things are protected within the digital world.

## 5 TAKE TURNS WITH YOUR FRIENDS

If you share technology with them, everyone can enjoy it equally. You'll also learn to respect the wishes of others, and we'll all be better people.

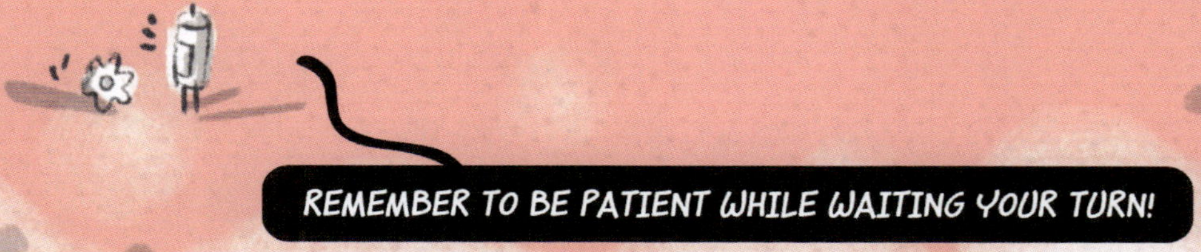

Technology is so wonderful
that sometimes it seems like magic..."

"As amazing as it may seem, remember:
the real magic is always created by...

# YOU.

APPENDIX

# GLOSSARY OF TERMS

Words help shape and color your ideas. They are like the building blocks that help you construct the world you imagine and where you would like to live.

Words are powerful!

That's why we're not leaving without giving you a list of all the new words you've just learned so you can gradually add them to your vocabulary.

**ALGORITHM** An algorithm is a set of precise steps or instructions followed to solve a problem or perform a specific task. They are essential in computers because they allow them to perform tasks efficiently and accurately.

**APPLICATIONS** An application or app is a program that you can use on your tablet or phone to play, learn, or do fun things.

**ARROW KEYS** The arrow keys or directional keys are the ones you use to move up, down, left, or right on the screen.

**BEEP** "Beep" is used as onomatopoeia to represent the sound generated by electronic devices when emitting an audible signal.

**BICYCLE** The bicycle is a means of transportation created by humans to move from one place to another efficiently and sustainably.

**BINARY** The binary system is a number system that only uses two digits, 0 and 1. Computers use it to process or work with information.

**BINARY WORLD** Zerus and Ona live in the Binary World, an exciting place inside the computer, where every day is a new adventure. They share their lives with many other zeros and ones, and together they take care of the computer's daily tasks.

**BITS** Bits are the basic unit of information in digital systems, representing a binary value of 0 or 1. They are like small switches inside computers, representing values of 0 (off) or 1 (on).

**BRUSH** In a drawing program, the brush is a function that simulates a real brush. It allows you to apply different strokes and effects as if it were a digital canvas.

**BUG** Code errors that may exist within a computer program are often called "bugs."

**BYTE** A byte is a set of 8 bits, which is the minimum amount of data that a computer can handle. Without bytes, most tasks on computers would be impossible to perform.

**CAPACITOR** Capacitors live inside computers. They are like small batteries that help maintain stable energy for it to function correctly.

**CHARACTER** A character is any letter, number, symbol, or space we use when writing on a computer.

**CHIP** Chips are Zerus and Ona's group of friends, and they accompany them in every task. Sometimes mischievous, and sometimes very useful and skilled, they don't miss a beat! In a computer, a chip is also called an electronic circuit.

**COLOR** The color function in a drawing program allows you to choose the tone and intensity of a color to apply it to the digital canvas.

**COMPUTER** Computers are machines that are all around us. They are very good at following instructions or steps stored in their memory.

**CURSOR** The cursor is a small symbol that blinks on the screen and indicates where the current position of a text is. It's like a marker that shows you where you can write or interact on the screen.

**DEBUG** The process of "debugging" involves finding and correcting any errors that may exist in a computer program.

**DELETE KEY** The delete key is a button you use to remove things on the computer.

**DESKTOP COMPUTER** These are computers designed to be used on a desktop. They are usually more powerful than a laptop.

**DIGITAL** We say that a tool or device is digital when it operates with numbers from the binary system, such as 0 and 1.

**DOUBLE CLICK** We double-click a mouse when we press the left button quickly twice to open or execute a file or program. It's like clapping your hands twice very fast!

**DOWNLOADS** The downloads folder is a place on your computer where files coming from the Internet or other devices are automatically saved. Once there, you can move and organize them as you wish in other folders.

**EMAIL** Email is an electronic communication system that allows you to send messages and files over the Internet between users with email addresses.

**ERASER** The eraser function removes strokes or specific areas of a drawing to correct mistakes or make adjustments to the design.

**FILE** A file is a set of data, such as text, images, music, or programs, that is saved under a unique name and can be accessed and manipulated as a single entity.

**FILL** The fill function allows you to fill closed areas of a drawing with a solid color or texture.

**FOLDER** A folder is like a box or basket where you can store and group many related files together to keep them organized and easily accessible.

**GADGET** A gadget is any small electronic device, like a smartwatch or a drone.

**GIGA** A gigabyte is a unit of measurement representing one billion bytes of data. For example, a movie can take up around 10 gigabytes.

**ICON** Icons are small images that represent something on the computer, like an application, a file, or a folder. You can click on some of them to open something, while others are just decorative.

**INBOX** It's like a digital mailbox where you can receive messages and emails from your friends and family.

**INFINITY** Infinity is more than just a large number; it's an idea that represents something that has no limit or end, like the universe or imagination.

**INPUT DEVICE** An input device is any device or tool that allows you to enter data or instructions into a computer.

**INTERNET** The Internet is a worldwide network of computers that allows people to communicate, share information, and access online services.

**KEY** Each button on a keyboard that you use to write and give instructions is called a key. Each key represents a character (letter, number, symbol) or a specific function.

**KEYBOARD** A keyboard is an input device. It consists of a set of keys that allow you to enter data and instructions into a computer.

**LAPTOP COMPUTER** A laptop computer is a compact and lightweight computer designed to be carried and used anywhere. It's called that because it fits on your lap!

**LED** LEDs are small lights that help us know if something is on or working in the computer. They are also used in some screens to show us images and colors.

**MEGA** A mega is a unit of information measurement that represents one million bytes. That's as big as a million characters!

**MEMORY** A computer's memory is like its brain, where it stores information to use when needed.

**MICROCHIPS** Microchips are small circuits inside the computer that process information and execute instructions as if they were tiny brains.

**MOUSE** The mouse is an input device for computers used to move the cursor on the screen and click on icons and options.

**ONA** Ona is a 1 bit that loves to dance, create colorful atoms, and potions to concentrate. When bored, she counts to infinity.

**OUTBOX** The outbox is where messages you want to send are saved, waiting to be delivered to their destination.

**OUTPUT DEVICE** An output device is any device or tool that displays information from a computer.

**PASSWORD** Passwords are secret words that protect important things, like your games or online accounts, so that only you can access them.

**PENCIL** We can say that a pencil is technology because it is a tool created by humans to perform a specific task: writing or drawing.

**PENCIL SHARPENER** A pencil sharpener is also technology because it is a tool designed to sharpen pencils, making their use easier and also making them last longer.

**PHONE** A phone is a device that allows you to talk, send messages, and use applications, like games or taking photos.

**PIGEON** Pigeons were once used as messengers to carry messages before phones and computers were invented.

**PIXEL** A pixel is a digital measurement unit and forms the images on a screen.

**PNG** PNG is a type of image file used to store high-quality images. Additionally, it supports transparency, so PNG images can have a transparent background that lets you see through it.

**POWERS OF TWO** Powers of two are numbers obtained by multiplying two by itself a certain number of times. For example: 2^0 = 1, 2^1 = 2, 2^2 = 4, 2^3 = 8, and so on. They are important in computer science and mathematics.

**PRINTER** A printer is an output device. It prints text or images on paper from data received from a computer or other device.

**PROGRAM** Computer programs are text files containing instructions that tell a computer what to do. Thanks to them, humans can give orders.

**RGB** RGB is a color model used in electronic devices, such as computer screens and TVs. It represents a wide range of colors by combining three primary components/colors: Red, Green, and Blue.

**ROBOT** A robot is a machine that can perform tasks automatically. They are everywhere, like in the supermarket, hospitals, and even inside your toys.

**SCISSORS** Scissors are also technology because they help us cut materials more precisely and easily.

**SCREEN** A screen is an output device. It displays visual information, such as text, images, or videos, generated by a computer.

**SHAPES AND LINES** It's common for drawing programs to allow you to create geometric shapes like circles, squares, and triangles, as well as straight or curved lines.

**SITES** On the Internet, a site is a place or set of related and linked pages where you can find information, images, videos, or other content.

**SPACE BAR** The space bar on a keyboard is the large key you use to leave a space between words when typing.

**SPEAKERS** Speakers are output devices. They produce sound, allowing you to hear audio generated by a computer or other device.

**SWIMMING GOGGLES** Swimming goggles are also technology because they protect our eyes and improve our vision underwater while swimming.

**TABLET** A tablet is like a small computer with a touchscreen where you can play, watch videos, and learn fun things.

**TAGS** Tags are keywords or categories associated with files, documents, or data to organize them.

**TASK** A task is a specific activity that the computer carries out, such as running a program, processing data, or performing a particular operation.

**TECH** "Tech" is an abbreviation of "technology".

**TECHNOLOGY** We call technology all the things that have been created by people to make our lives easier and help us live better.

**THICKNESS** We can also define how large we want the stroke of a brush to be in a drawing program. This is the thickness of the brush and is usually measured in pixels.

**TOOL** In computing, a tool is any program or device that helps perform specific tasks.

**TOOTHBRUSH** Whiz-Bang Technology! The toothbrush is a tool designed to clean teeth effectively, helping to keep your mouth healthy and clean.

**TOUCHPAD** The touchpad is a touch-sensitive surface that allows you to interact with the screen through gestures, such as tapping, swiping, or pinching to control and navigate the device without needing an external mouse or keyboard. For example, laptops have a touchscreen instead of a mouse.

**TRASH** It's where files you delete are temporarily stored. Later on, you can decide whether to delete them permanently or recover them.

**TYPE** We use the verb "type" when referring to pressing the keys on a keyboard to write or enter information into a computer.

**USERNAME** The username is like a special nickname you use to log into your account on a computer for the computer to know it's you.

**WHEEL** The wheel is one of humanity's greatest technological inventions. It helps us in transportation, industry, agriculture, and construction, reducing human effort in tasks such as moving heavy loads.

**XEROX STAR 8010** The Xerox Star 8010 was one of the first commercially marketed desktop computers as an integrated office system in the 1980s. It incorporated advanced features such as a graphical user interface, a mouse, and a set of productivity applications.

**ZERUS** Zerus is a 0 bit that loves mixing colors, creating algorithms, and dreams of traveling to space by bicycle.

STAY IN THE LOOP ABOUT THE UPCOMING TITLES IN THE COLLECTION:

Digital Artist

Let's get Coding!

We are Connected

Here we go, Robotics!

Amazing Intelligence

We Navigate Safely

EPILOGUE

# A JOURNEY TO DIGITAL UNDERSTANDING

Zerus & Ona's mission is to bring the understanding of computing to every child on the planet.

Because understanding technology is everyone's task. Only then can we master it, not the other way around.

This book is the first of an exciting collection that will address various computer topics. Upcoming titles will cover concepts of programming, data and information, the Internet and networks...

Our goal is to provide an introduction to each of these topics in an easy, fun, and accessible way for everyone.

To stay updated on the latest news and receive exclusive content, we invite you to join our newsletter.

Visit www.zerusandona.com to subscribe.

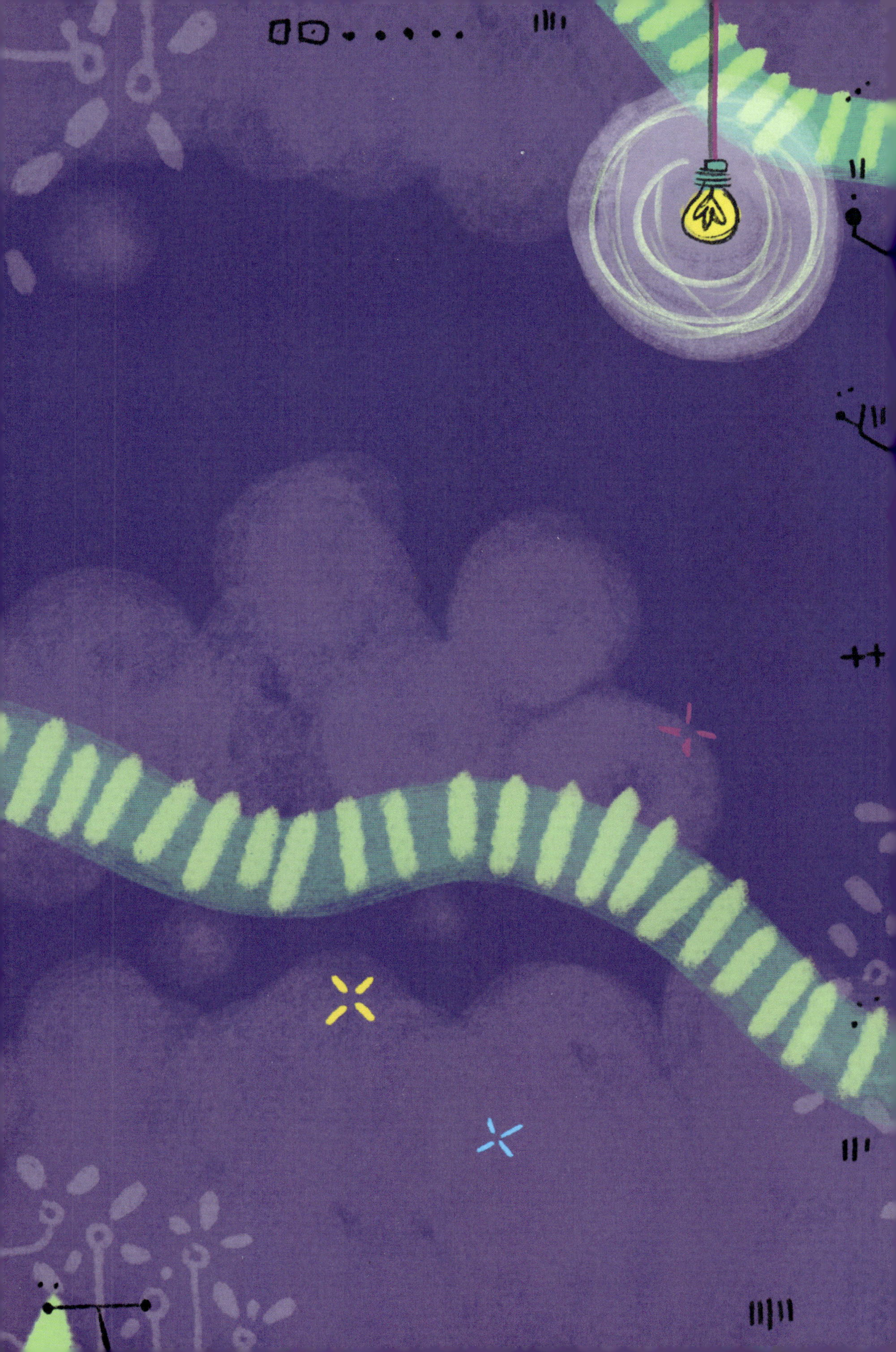

Printed by Amazon Italia Logistica S.r.l.
Torrazza Piemonte (TO), Italy

60496138R00051